# remember when...?

Remember Catch-22 and The Feminine Mystique?
When Haight Ashbury was the center of the universe?
How about the Singing Nun, or Zap Comix?
Can you remember when psychedlic light shows
were common, or when surfing was uncommonly cool?
When 'England swings like a pendulum do'?

## then you must be ready for a 60s party!

THIS BOOK OF MEMORIES PRESENTED TO:

_____

ON THE OCCASION OF:

_____

DATE:

# Setting the scene

## 1960
- Four Black Americans stage a sit-in at Woolworth's whites-only lunch counter
- The first Playboy Club opens in Chicago
- The first birth control pill is approved by the FDA

## 1961
- JFK establishes the Peace Corps
- Russian ballet dancer Rudolph Nureyev defects to the West while performing in Paris
- The Berlin Wall is built to stop the exodus of East Germans to West Germany

## 1962
- The World's Fair opens in Seattle, featuring the Space Needle

## 1963
- Martin Luther King, Jr. gives his "I have a dream" speech at the Lincoln Memorial in Washington D.C.
- Four black girls are killed when a bomb explodes in a Birmingham, Alabama church
- JFK is assassinated in Dallas, Texas
- Lee Harvey Oswald is shot to death by Jack Ruby, as millions watch on TV
- The five-digit zip code is adopted by the US Post Office to speed mail sorting

## 1964
- Ford officially introduces the Mustang
- New York hosts the World's Fair
- Martin Luther King, Jr. is awarded the Nobel Peace Prize
- The Beatles are on the Ed Sullivan Show, and Beatlemania grips the world

## 1965
- A massive blackout in New York City, five states, and parts of Canada leaves 30 million without electricity

## 1966
- The National Organization for Women is founded
- Mao Tse-Tung launches the Cultural Revolution, which destroys all traces of Western culture
- Apartheid policy becomes state-sanctioned in South Africa

## 1967

❖ The Beatles release *Sgt. Pepper's Lonely Hearts Club Band*
❖ In the Six Days War, Israeli forces defeat an invasion by Egypt, Syria and Jordan
❖ World's first human heart transplant is performed by Dr. Christiaan Barnard in Capetown, South Africa
❖ *Rolling Stone* magazine begins publication

## 1968

❖ Soviet troops invade Czechoslovakia to end the liberal regime of Dubcek
❖ Assassinations stun the nation: Martin Luther King, Jr. in Memphis; Robert F. Kennedy in Los Angeles
❖ Richard M. Nixon wins the US presidency

## 1969

❖ American, Neil Armstrong, is the first man on the moon
❖ The first outdoor rock festival, Woodstock, attracts more than 300,000
❖ Britain sends troops to Northern Ireland to police unrest between the Catholic minority and the Protestant majority

**THE BUZZ**

Andy Warhol
Robert Crumb (comics)
Sit-in
Hippies
Flower Power
Counter-culture
Communes
The beautiful people
Make Love, Not War
The Red Guard
Transcendental Meditation (Maharishi Mahesh Yogi)
Woodstock Nation
Summer of Love
Conscientious objector
The Establishment

SAVE THE LAST DANCE FOR ME > The Drifters • I FALL TO PIECES > Patsy Cline • CRYIN' > Roy Orbison • BLOWIN' IN THE

UNDER THE BOARDWALK > The Drifters • A HARD DAY'S NIGHT > The Beatles • DIZZY > Tommy Roe • PROUD MARY >

TO SIR WITH LOVE > Lulu • HAPPY TOGETHER > The Turtles • WINDY > The Association • LIGHT MY FIRE > The Doors •

SUMMER IN THE CITY > Lovin' Spoonful • BALLAD OF THE GREEN BERETS > Sgt. Barry Sadler • CHERISH > The Association •

LOVE IS BLUE > Paul Mauriat • THE DOCK OF THE BAY > Otis Redding • DANCE TO THE MUSIC > Sly & the Family Stone •

DOWNTOWN > Petula Clark • MRS. BROWN YOU'VE GOT A LOVELY DAUGHTER > Herman's Hermits • I GOT YOU BABE > Sonny & Cher

THE LION SLEEPS TONIGHT > Tokens • THE HOUSE OF THE RISING SUN > Animals • THE LOCO-MOTION

MY GENERATION > The Who

Joan Baez
Dave Clark Five
The Kingston Trio
The Hungry-I

feedback
Janis Joplin
Traffic

Mersey Sound
The Grateful Dead
Ten Years After

THE BUZZ

Mod
Berry Gordy
Zap Comix
James Brown

Light Show
Tamla Motown
Swinging Sixties

# charts

WHERE THE BOYS ARE > Connie Francis • THE TWIST > Chubby Checker • I CAN'T STOP LOVING YOU > Ray Charles
WIND > Peter, Paul & Mary • I WANT TO HOLD YOUR HAND > The Beatles • SHE LOVES YOU > The Beatles
Credence Clearwater Revival • WHITE RABBIT > Jefferson Airplane • BORN TO BE WILD > Steppenwolf
WIPEOUT > The Surfaris • SATISFACTION > The Rolling Stones • WOOLY BULLY > Sam the Sham & the Pharoahs
WHEN A MAN LOVE A WOMAN > Percy Sledge • HANKY PANKY > Tommy James & the Shondells • RESPECT > Aretha Franklin
AQUARIUS > Fifth Dimension • CALIFORNIA DREAMIN' > Mamas & the Papas • LAST TRAIN TO CLARKSVILLE > The Monkees
• STOP! IN THE NAME OF LOVE > The Supremes • THIS DIAMOND RING > Gary Lewis & the Playboys •
> Little Eva • SURFIN' USA > The Beach Boys • WILD THING > The Troggs • TELSTAR > The Tornados •
UPTIGHT (EVERYTHING'S ALL RIGHT) > Stevie Wonder • HEY JOE > Jimi Hendrix • EIGHT MILES HIGH > The Byrds

## care to dance?

The Watusi

The Mashed Potato

The Hitch Hike

The Monkey          The Dog          The Frug

The Freddie

The Swim          The Twist          The Pony

The LocoMotion

The Hanky-Panky

The Jerk

MUSIC

1960s

4

The Andy Griffith Show

The Untouchables  The Twilight Zone

The Donna Reed Show

Dennis the Menace

Peyton Place

WE LOVED OUR

TV

Rowan & Martin's Laugh-In

Bonanza  I Spy

Star Trek  The Avengers

The Fugitive  The Flintstones

The Beverly Hillbillies

My Three Sons  Car 54, Where Are You?

The Dick Van Dyke Show  McHale's Navy

Wide World of Sports  The Smothers Brothers Comedy Hour

My Favorite Martian  Sesame Street

Petticoat Junction  I Dream of Jeannie  60 Minutes

Flipper  The Dating Game

Bewitched  Get Smart  The Mod Squad

The Monkees

Gilligan's Island  Hogan's Heroes  Julia

The Addams Family  The Flying Nun  The Brady Bunch

# slang of the 60s

Keep on Truckin'

Don't trust anyone over 30!

A Gas

Bummer

Go Ape

Church Key

Boogie

Bread

Crash

Dig It

The Fuzz/Pigs

Stoned

Far Out, Man

Freak

Kipe

Lay It On Me

My Old Lady/Old Man

Outta Sight

## THE BUZZ

Uncle Jesten

Marijuana

Cruising

Free Love

Consciousness Raising

UC Berkeley

glasspacks

Peace Sign

Flower Child

No Meat on Fridays

Cultural Revolution

Global Village

Women's Lib

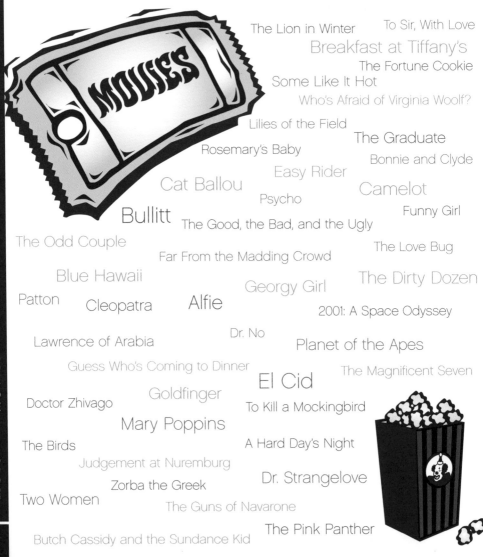

MOVIES

The Lion in Winter    To Sir, With Love
Breakfast at Tiffany's
The Fortune Cookie
Some Like It Hot
Who's Afraid of Virginia Woolf?
Lilies of the Field
The Graduate
Rosemary's Baby    Bonnie and Clyde
Easy Rider
Cat Ballou    Camelot
Psycho    Funny Girl
Bullitt    The Good, the Bad, and the Ugly
The Odd Couple    The Love Bug
Far From the Madding Crowd
Blue Hawaii    The Dirty Dozen
Georgy Girl
Patton    Cleopatra    Alfie    2001: A Space Odyssey
Dr. No
Lawrence of Arabia    Planet of the Apes
Guess Who's Coming to Dinner    The Magnificent Seven
El Cid
Goldfinger
Doctor Zhivago    To Kill a Mockingbird
Mary Poppins
The Birds    A Hard Day's Night
Judgement at Nuremburg
Zorba the Greek    Dr. Strangelove
Two Women
The Guns of Navarone
The Pink Panther
Butch Cassidy and the Sundance Kid

# academy award® best pictures

I Am Curious – Yellow

The Great Escape

Spartacus

La Dolce Vita

Advise and Consent

The Longest Day

Exodus

### THE BUZZ

Marcello Mastroianni

Brigitte Bardot

Rock Hudson & Doris Day

Sophia Loren

Anne Bancroft & Patty Duke

Vanessa Redgrave

Paul Newman & Joanne Woodward

Steve McQueen

Anthony Quinn

Jean-Paul Belmondo

Elizabeth Taylor & Richard Burton

Jean Seberg

Lynn Redgrave

Mutiny on the Bounty

Hud

The Unsinkable Molly Brown

The Wild Bunch   The Greatest Story Ever Told

It's a Mad, Mad, Mad, Mad World

Barefoot in the Park

The Agony and the Ecstasy

MOVIES

1960s

8

# on broadway

CABARET

★

HOW TO SUCCEED
IN BUSINESS
WITHOUT REALLY
TRYING

★

HELLO, DOLLY!

★

MAME

★

MAN OF
LA MANCHA

★

FIDDLER ON
THE ROOF

★

SWEET CHARITY

★

A LITTLE NIGHT
MUSIC

★

THE GAY LIFE

★

CAMELOT

★

I CAN GET IT FOR
YOU WHOLESALE

★

1776

★

HAIR

★

THE FANTASTICKS

★

THE MIRACLE
WORKER

★

PROMISES,
PROMISES

★

# ON THE BOOKSHELF

SILENT SPRING · Rachel Carson

BE HERE NOW · Ram Dass

CATCH-22 · Joseph Heller

BLACK LIKE ME · John H. Griffin

ONE FLEW OVER THE CUCKOO'S NEST · Ken Kesey

BORN FREE · Joy Adamson

THE BELL JAR · Sylvia Plath

TO KILL A MOCKINGBIRD · Harper Lee

TURN ON, TUNE IN, DROP OUT · Timothy Leary

THE VALLEY OF THE DOLLS · Jacqueline Susann

THE STRAWBERRY STATEMENT: NOTES OF A COLLEGE REVOLUTIONARY

2001: A SPACE ODYSSEY · Arthur C. Clarke

THE MEDIUM IS THE MESSAGE · Marshall McLuhan

SLAUGHTERHOUSE FIVE · Kurt Vonnegut

THE FEMININE MYSTIQUE · Betty Friedan

THE ELECTRIC KOOL-AID ACID TEST · Tom Wolfe

UNSAFE AT ANY SPEED · Ralph Nader

IN COLD BLOOD · Truman Capote

WHOLE EARTH CATALOG · Stewart Brand, ed.

AUTOBIOGRAPHY OF MALCOLM X

THE GROUP · Mary McCarthy

# WHERE WERE YOU

## 1960
- John F. Kennedy is the first Catholic to win the White House
- A US U-2 spy plane is shot down over Soviet territory
- Seventeen African nations win independence from European colonial powers

## 1961
- The US breaks diplomatic ties with Cuba when Castro accuses the US of plotting against it
- Freedom Riders—civil rights workers—travel through the South in an effort to have federal law enforced

## 1962
- US combat troops are sent to aid South Vietnamese forces against the Communist North Vietnamese insurgents
- After JFK imposes a blockade of Cuba, Soviet nuclear missiles are withdrawn, and nuclear war is averted
- John Glenn becomes the first American to orbit the earth
- James Meredith, a black air force veteran, succeeds in enrolling at the U of Mississippi

## 1963
- Dogs and fire hoses are turned on civil rights demonstrators in Birmingham, Alabama
- A hotline between Washington and Moscow is established to prevent delays that might result in accidental nuclear war

## 1964
- The Vietnam war escalates under President Johnson, after an alleged attack on US ships in the Gulf of Tonkin
- The Civil Rights Act is passed by Congress
- In the Soviet Union, Nikita Krushchev is ousted and is replaced by Leonid Brezhnev
- Lyndon Johnson is re-elected over Barry Goldwater in a landslide victory

## 1965
- Malcolm X is assassinated at a rally in Harlem
- The Medicare bill is signed into law
- A clash between white police and black residents in Watts escalates into a 5-day riot
- Lyndon Johnson signs the Voting Rights Act into law

# WHEN...?

## 1966

• Cigarette packages begin carrying the Surgeon General's warning
• The Supreme Court rules that criminals must be advised of their rights, in the Miranda case
• Eight student nurses are stabbed and strangled by Richard Speck
• A student at the University of Texas shoots 44 people from a campus tower

## 1968

• The success of the Communist Tet offensive stuns Americans
• The USS Pueblo, a navy spy ship, is seized by North Korean gunboats in international waters
• The Civil Rights Act is signed by President Johnson
• Students at Columbia University take over campus buildings to protest the university's involvement with the Pentagon
• During the Democratic National Convention in Chicago, a riot leaves more than one thousand injured

## 1969

• Sen. Edward Kennedy drives his car off a bridge on Chappaquiddick Island; his passenger dies in the accident
• Cult leader Charles Manson and his followers are charged with the grisly murders of actress Sharon Tate and others

## 1967

• Apollo 1 astronauts die when a flash fire breaks out in the spacecraft during testing
• Elvis Presley weds Priscilla Beaulieu in Las Vegas
• Thurgood Marshall becomes the first black appointed to the Supreme Court
• Antiwar demonstrators numbered at 150,000 gather at the Lincoln Memorial in Washington DC to protest the Vietnam war

## THE BUZZ

Red China
Black Power
My Lai
Caesar Chavez
Black Panthers
Abbie Hoffman
PT-109
Malcolm X
The Weathermen
The Chicago Seven
Napalm
Black Muslims
Draft card burning
The Great Society
Bay of Pigs
James Earl Ray
Civil rights
Paris Peace Talks

# what we wore

Headbands

Courréges boots

culottes

Geometric designs

Granny dresses

miniskirts

go-go boots

buttons with sayings on them

plastic clothing

tight-fitting men's pants

baby-doll look

Wide ties

fishnet stockings

See-through blouses

Batik

long hair on men

Peasant skirts

frilled cuffs on men – edwardian look

Straight hair

Nehru jackets

Cutoffs

False eyelashes

The gypsy look

Pink

Love beads

Granny glasses

Fringed vests and jackets

Bouffant hairdos

Tie-dye

Velvets, ribbons, and ruffles

Wedges (shoes)

Big zippers

## POPULAR VACATION DESTINATIONS

**Europe**
**London**
**India**
**Hawaii**

## THE BUZZ

Aluminum Christmas Trees
op art
Trimline phone
Unisex

Carnaby Street
Easy Bake toy oven
Jean Shrimpton

Peter Max
Topless bathing suits
Mods vs. Rockers

Yardley
Lava lamp
Vidal Sassoon
Twiggy

Beanbag chairs
Skateboards
Troll dolls

## If you had wheels, you had to drive a...

vw beetle or bus
american motors ambassador
opel kadett
plymouth fury
chevrolet impala
ford mustang
ford falcon
mercury cougar
triumph spitfire
chevrolet camaro

**food trends**

Total® cereal
Sprite®
McDonald's® Big Mac™
Coq au Vin
French cooking
Fresca®
Frosted Mini Wheats®
Diet Pepsi®
Boil in the bag veggies from Green Giant®
Freeze-dried instant coffee
Granola
Vegetarianism
casseroles
Beef Wellington
Apple Jacks® cereal
Carrot cake
Pop-Tarts®
Chocolate Mousse
fondue
A&W® Drive-In
SpaghettiOs®
Julia Child
Bac-Os®
Campbell's® Chunky™ Soups

# Shrimp Cocktail

**1/2 cup** ketchup
**1/2 cup** cocktail sauce
**1 Tbsp.** bottled horseradish
**1 tsp.** Worcestershire sauce

Mix well and serve with medium or large shelled, de-veined cooked shrimp.

# who won? THE WORLD SERIES

**1960** ...................Pittsburgh Pirates 4, New York Yankees 3

**1961** ...........................New York Yankees 4, Cincinnati Reds 1

**1962** ..........New York Yankees 4, San Francisco Giants 3

**1963** ........Los Angeles Dodgers 4, New York Yankees 0

**1964** ................St. Louis Cardinals 4, New York Yankees 3

**1965** ..............Los Angeles Dodgers 4, Minnesota Twins 3

**1966** ...........Baltimore Orioles 4, Los Angeles Dodgers 0

**1967** ...............St. Louis Cardinals 4, Boston Red Sox 3

**1968** ........................Detroit Tigers 4, St. Louis Cardinals 3

**1969** ...................New York Mets 4, Baltimore Orioles 1

# who won? THE STANLEY CUP

**1960** .........Montreal Canadiens 4, Toronto Maple Leafs 3

**1961** ..............Chicago Blackhawks 4, Detroit Red Wings 2

**1962** .......Toronto Maple Leafs 4, Chicago Blackhawks 2

**1963** ................Toronto Maple Leafs 4, Detroit Red Wings 1

**1964** ..............Toronto Maple Leafs 4, Detroit Red Wings 3

**1965** .......Montreal Canadiens 4, Chicago Blackhawks 3

**1966** ...............Montreal Canadiens 4, Detroit Red Wings 2

**1967** .........Toronto Maple Leafs 4, Montreal Canadiens 2

**1968** ........................Montreal Canadiens 4, St. Louis Blues 0

**1969** ........................Montreal Canadiens 4, St. Louis Blues 0

## THE NBA CHAMPIONSHIP

**1960**
Boston Celtics 4
St. Louis Hawks 3

**1961**
Boston Celtics 4
St. Louis Hawks 1

**1962**
Boston Celtics 4
Los Angeles Lakers 2

**1963**
Boston Celtics 4
Los Angeles Lakers 2

**1964**
Boston Celtics 4
San Francisco Warriors 1

**1965**
Boston Celtics 4
Los Angeles Lakers 1

**1966**
Boston Celtics 4
Los Angeles Lakers 3

**1967**
Philadelphia 76ers 4 San
Francisco Warriors 2

**1968**
Boston Celtics 4
Los Angeles Lakers 2

**1969**
Boston Celtics 4
Los Angeles Lakers 3

# who won?

# THE NFL OR AFL CHAMPIONSHIP/SUPERBOWL

| | |
|---|---|
| **1960** | Philadelphia Eagles 17, Green Bay Packers 13 – NFL |
| 1961 | Houston Oilers 10, San Diego Chargers 3 – AFL |
| | Green Bay Packers 37, New York Giants 0 – NFL |
| **1962** | Dallas Texans 20, Houston Oilers 17 – AFL |
| | Green Bay Packers 16, New York Giants 7 – NFL |
| 1963 | San Diego Chargers 51, Boston Patriots 10 – AFL |
| | Chicago Bears 14, New York Giants 10 – NFL |
| **1964** | Buffalo Bills 20, San Diego Chargers 7 – AFL |
| | Cleveland Browns 27, Baltimore Colts 0 – NFL |
| 1965 | Buffalo Bills 23, San Diego Chargers 0 – AFL |
| | Green Bay Packers 23, Cleveland Browns 12 – NFL |
| **1966** | Kansas City Chiefs 31, Buffalo Bills 7 – AFL |
| | Green Bay Packers 34, Dallas Texans 27 – NFL |
| 1967 | The first Super Bowl: |
| | Green Bay Packers 35, Kansas City Chiefs 10 |
| **1968** | Green Bay Packers 33, Oakland Raiders 14 |
| 1969 | New York Jets 16, Baltimore Colts 7 |

THE BUZZ

Vince Lombardi
Al Oerter
Bobby Hull
Broadway Joe
Jack Nicklaus
Peggy Fleming
Sandy Koufax
Mario Andretti
Fosbury Flop
Boston Celtics
Bob Beamon

1960s

**1960**
- Summer Olympic Games are held in Rome, Italy; Cassius Clay wins the light-heavyweight gold medal
- Running barefoot in the marathon, Abebe Bikila of Ethiopia becomes the first black African Olympic champion
- Wilma Rudolph, who had polio as a child, wins three gold medals in track
- Winter Games are held in Squaw Valley, California

**1961**
- The World Figure Skating Championships canceled after the entire United States team dies in a plane crash

**1962**
- Rod Laver wins the men's Grand Slam in tennis
- Arnold Palmer wins the Masters Tournament, as he did in '61
- Jackie Robinson becomes the first black American to be inducted into the Baseball Hall of Fame

**1963**
- The Pro Football Hall of Fame opens in Canton, Ohio, with 17 charter members

**1964**
- Cassius Clay, later known as Muhammad Ali, wins the World Heavyweight Boxing Championship, beating Sonny Liston
- Tokyo, Japan, hosts the Summer Olympics, the first to be held in Asia
- American swimmer Don Schollander win four gold medals
- Winter Olympic Games open in Innsbruck, Austria

**1965**
- United States wins the Ryder Cup 19 ¹/₂ to 12 ¹/₂ over Britain in world team golf

**1966**
- England defeats Germany to win the World Cup Final
- American runner Jim Ryun sets a new world record for the mile at 3:51.3

**1967**
- Muhammed Ali is stripped of his World Heavyweight Champion titles and banned from boxing for his refusal to be inducted into the US Army
- The first World Cup tour in Alpine skiing is organized for the three ski events, "Downhill," "Slalom," and "Giant Slalom"
- The First Super Bowl is held
- Billie Jean King sweeps American and British women's singles, doubles and mixed doubles championships

**1968**
- Summer Olympics are held in the thin air of Mexico City, Mexico, disastrous for athletes competing in endurance events
- Olympic timing is done manually and electronically, but for the first time, the electronic time is considered official
- During the US national anthem, two American runners raise their fists in a Black Power salute
- Jean-Claude Killy wins the Triple Crown of Alpine Skiing at the Winter Olympics in Grenoble, France

**1969**
- The Bolivian world cup soccer team is killed in a plane crash near La Paz, Bolivia
- Australian Rod Laver, one of only two men to ever win the Grand Slam in tennis, wins it for the second time

a decade of sports

# LIFE JUST WOULDN'T BE THE SAME WITHOUT...

CPR, A METHOD OF SAVING HEART ATTACK VICTIMS

ELECTRIC TOOTHBRUSH

LASERS

PUSHBUTTON PHONES

LEGO® BRICKS

COLOR TV

FELT TIP PEN

COCA-COLA® IN CANS

ASTROTURF

THE CONCORDE SUPERSONIC AIRLINER

LYCRA® (A SPANDEX FIBER)

POLAROID® COLOR FILM

IBM® SELECTRIC TYPEWRITER

MICROWAVE OVENS

GATORADE®

COFFEEMATE®

JACUZZI WHIRLPOOL BATHS (HOT TUBS)

WATERBEDS

THE MEASLES VACCINE

# checklist for the perfect party

**THREE WEEKS BEFORE:**

- [ ] Plan the occasion > *a 60s nostalgia party*
- [ ] Create a compatible guest list
- [ ] Choose a location that will accommodate the number of guests
- [ ] Send invitations [date, time (start/end), place, directions] > *Ask guests to dress in clothing of the era*
- [ ] Plan and select decorations > *This can include old yearbooks, record albums and other memorabilia*
- [ ] Begin collecting materials and creating props
  > *Visit garage sales for old 45s and LPs, even old clothes*   > *Movie memorabilia stores are good sources*
- [ ] Prepare menu and grocery list  > *Consider using food from the era for extra nostalgia*
- [ ] Select and hire caterer/serving help (if using)

**A FEW DAYS BEFORE:**

- [ ] Call any guests who have not responded
- [ ] Buy groceries and beverages
- [ ] Prepare and refrigerate/freeze food items that can be made in advance
- [ ] Make party costume or select outfit

**ONE DAY BEFORE:**

- [ ] Clean house, party room facility or other party site
- [ ] Set up and arrange party room
- [ ] Thaw out frozen party foods
- [ ] Get out serving pieces
- [ ] Coordinate last-minute arrangements with caterer, servers (if using)

**THE DAY OF:**

- [ ] Decorate party room
- [ ] Prepare and arrange remaining food
- [ ] Coordinate set-up, service, cleanup with hired helpers (if using)
- [ ] Mentally travel through party  > *BEGINNING: arrivals and introductions*   > *MIDDLE: food and activities; have everyone sign the book*   > *END: wrap it up! Party favors, Polaroid photos*
- [ ] Dress in party outfit
- [ ] Await guests
- [ ] Have a good time!

# happy day!

:)

## HOPE YOU ENJOYED YOUR PARTY...
## WE SURE DID!